DR. SEBI FASTING

A royal road to Healing by fasting and losing weight through Dr. Sebi Alkaline Diet (Plant-Based Diet, mucus less diet)

Carin C. Hendry

Copyright

No part of this book may be reproduced, transmitted or stored in a retrieval system in any form or by any means, electronic, mechanical, recording or otherwise without the prior permission of the author.

Dedication

This book is especially dedicated to everyone wanting get total cure from herpes virus without going for none feasible cure and expensive drugs that does not really work.

Table of Content

Copyright 3

Dedication 4

Introduction 10

Plenty of the wrong food diet 12

Spring purify fasting to cleanse the body 13

Wrong thinking brings illness 14

Illness mindset 15

The simple way of dieting 17

How I got sick 18

Disharmony brings a host of suffering and diseases 20

Discipline for good health 20

The laws of life 21

Nature signs of an illness 22

Wise self-healing 23

Purifying the body by fasting, a thorough cleansing 24

CHAPTER 1 26

Unique ways to eat clean from the nutritional guide Dr. Sebi diet food list - Fruits and veggies 26

How to eat clean from the nutritional guide 26

Healthy Eating Morning Meals From Dr. Sebi Nutritional Guide . 29

Natural Spring Water 30

Natural Living Meals Upon Waking Up In The Morning 31

The Difference In Fruits And Vegetables 32

When To Eat Fresh Fruits 34

When To Eat Vegetables 35

CHAPTER 2 37

Best Ways To Get Rid Of Phlegm After Eating And Clear Mucus From The Throat 37

What is mucus? 39

Difference Between Phlegm And Mucus 40

Phlegm Carries Disease 41

The Relation Between Food And Disease 42

Mucus disease 42

Mucus Is The Cause Of Every Disease - Dr. Sebi 43

Mucus And Phlegm Cause Disease 44

Phlegm After Eating 47

Symptoms Of Constant Mucus In The Throat 49

Natural Remedies To Clear Mucus 50

Natural remedies for phlegm 52

Herbs for mucus and phlegm relief 54

Mucusless diet and Mucus relief .. 55

CHAPTER 3 60

Benefits of fasting as recommended by Dr. Sebi 60

CHAPTER 4 70

Foods During Fasting 70

What Type Of Fasting Foods To Eat 71

Dr. Sebi Fasting Foods Checklist .73

The Fasting Foods To Eat 75

Vegetables to eat during fasting? .76

CHAPTER 5 78

How To Fast Safely To Remove Mucus, Toxins, And Lose Weight 78

What Is Fasting? 78

Before you fast 79

Why should you fast 80

What fasting will do 81

What about Water fasting 83

How to prepare for fasting 84

How long should you fast? 86

Fast to cleanse toxins....................87

How do you break a fast 89

Conclusion 91

Other Books By Carin C. Hendry 92

DR. SEBI FASTING

Introduction

A diet with inconsistent quantity and quality will do the body more harm from good. This can result in chronic diseases, excessive mucus discharge, and ill sufferings. With the widespread of world hunger, several cities with little to no support have taken to fasting. Fasting is unduly associated with hunger, and some individuals seem to think malnourishment and extreme hunger synonymous with some African countries is as a result of fasting. Research has proven that even when there is plenty of food to go around, people still fall ill due to undernourishment or total lack of nourishment. Ironically, when there is a shortage of food, chronic diseases, and other illnesses reduces drastically.

When a person goes on a weight loss journey, not only does such a person shed excess body mass, they also expel illnesses and diseases in the body such as diabetes, appendicitis, stomach illnesses, and nerve complaints.

Plenty of the wrong food diet

Interestingly, a high percentage of all known diseases and sicknesses are borne as a result of improper nourishment. Fasting seems to be the only way out when people fall victim to over-nourishment, improper diet, tobacco, and alcohol. According to Dick Gregory, his idea of proper nutrition is having plenty of food to eat regardless of what the menu looks like. It didn't take long for him to figure out he got things all wrong and mixed up as he was privileged to come across renowned natural living expert Dr. Alvenia Fulton who taught Dick how to fast and cleanse out excess mucus in his body effectively.

Spring purify fasting to cleanse the body

Everyday cooking and natural food give us the much-needed pleasure our taste buds crave, but things can turn bad real quick if we keep on repeating dietary mistakes. World-renowned herbalist, Dr. Sebi, said, "Healthy living, drinking natural spring water, and electric alkaline foods can keep the soul and body together." In addition to this, the idea of excellent eating is one that follows the rhythm of nature. A dieting ideology which strongly supports fasting once a year in order to prevent illnesses. This is mostly regarded as the royal road to healing.

Wrong thinking brings illness

There is a wrong notion in the minds of individuals living in countries where food is surplus as well as those in countries experiencing food scarcity – this notion is one that supports the school of thought that a fattening diet strengthens the body's defenses against diseases and illnesses. In Africa, being excessively chubby is seen as a sign of good living, which is envied by everyone. Being big is also attributed to wealth and having a special status.

Illness mindset

This way of thinking is totally wrong as there are known

consequences that walk hand-in-hand with being overfed, and these include eczema, cancer, gout, and rheumatism. Scientifically, it is a fact that overfed people are more prone to diseases and other lesser-known illnesses. This is not so for slim people whose diet is mainly vegetarian. The effects are there for all to see, and only those who genuinely obey the laws of nature, one of which adapting an alkaline-based plant diet, is key, live a more abundant life, and have fewer diseases.

The simple way of dieting

People who truly know what fasting is all about switch totally to a vegetarian diet. These sets of individuals are less likely to contract diseases like diabetes, gout, high blood pressure, eczema, etc. On the other hand, those of the school of thought that excess body fat is what keeps illnesses away from them will have a hard time staying healthy as their body has been fed with the wrong quality and quantity of food.

How I got sick

Time enslavement, technology, and a busy career. Letting an unauthentic living standards rule my life took my body out of rhythm. The rhythm of my biological clock was in total jeopardy. All my life, I had been anxious, time-restricted, nervous, eating wrongly, and with little to no exercise. All of these contributed immensely to the various kinds of diseases that plagued me.

My body's metabolism alarmingly slowed down due to my excessive intake of tobacco and alcohol. This hindered my body from healing itself, maintaining a balance, and fighting off illnesses of all kinds. I am not necessarily the one here, but so many of us are so entangle to our careers and businesses and in the process forget to take good care of our health.

Disharmony brings a host of suffering and diseases

The glands, tissues, and other vital organs of the body have been disharmonized. Toxic substances have overridden my entire body, and the after-effects are noticeable and glaring in my blood vessels and the body's ability to process energy. This lifestyle left me with a body full of toxic substances.

Discipline for good health

Am I the only one or is "most of our suffering from pain-staking diseases are the fruits of our desires," Dr. Sebi. To totally stop the intake of an entirely wrong diet, courage and strong will-power are needed as these substances damage our health.

The laws of life

Everyone must come to the realization that our body is under the laws of nature, which must not be broken for any reason. When we go against nature's nutrition order, our health suffers a setback. This setback leads to acute and chronic diseases, the realization of fasting then dwells upon us.

Nature signs of an illness

Naturally, when a disease creeps into the body, there are signs of backing this up and alert you about the impending danger. Loss of appetite is one of nature's ways of telling you there is a need to make a quick check on your health. According to Dr. Africa, this is so because "fasting is recognized as nature's healing apparatus." Loss of appetite is a crystal clear warning that the body's defense mechanism is weak. Other signals from nature when the body has fallen ill include vomiting, diarrhea, and sweating. All these are all indications that the body needs abstinence from food (i.e., fasting) to trigger its natural healing abilities.

Wise self-healing

According to Dr. Lailla, "the wise self-healing power of our body has superior capabilities that even the most qualified physician cannot perform miraculously artistically the way our body is capable of doing it." Yes, it's as simple as that. The art of eliminating chronic diseases is simply to fast with fruit juice or alkaline tea for intestinal cleansing to get rid of acute diseases such as influenza, scarlet fever, diphtheria, pneumonia, and tonsillitis, etc.

Purifying the body by fasting, a thorough cleansing

I will finish my presentation here without concluding how I started. I got sick because I violated the laws of nature; in turn, nature punished me with chronic diseases. Now, I must correct my mistakes by obeying the laws of nature. I have to cleanse myself, purify my body, and I have to rebuild it by undergoing deep cleansing. Like nature, the path of healing is represented by fasting to preserve the body of my immortal soul.

CHAPTER 1

Unique ways to eat clean from the nutritional guide Dr. Sebi diet food list - Fruits and veggies

How to eat clean from the nutritional guide

This is a structured daily meal plan for Dr. Sebi nutritional food guide. The structure for cultivating the habit of eating fresh fruit, vegetables, grains, and nuts that the great healer taught before his demise, fruits and vegetables are more important.

You can take a look at the full list of foods recommended by Dr. Sebi here:
(https://www.amazon.com/dp/B07RXLZ8VN

). I have learned about life in the last few years, and I have read books about holistic living, but the most important thing here is the natural life and a healthy lifestyle. My passion is to live as naturally as possible. Therefore, I feel that my first big step should be with myself and with what I eat. I have here Dr. Sebi's nutritional guide, and here's how to set up the list of alkaline electric foods.

One last point, if you have not heard of the nutritional guide before, it is an exhaustive list of organic alkaline foods that grow naturally in nature. These are not genetically modified foods but are rich in natural minerals. Food is electric, which complements our body because the body is electric. Finally, food supplements the biological structure of our body because they have what Dr. Sebi calls "chemical infinity."

Healthy Eating Morning Meals From Dr. Sebi Nutritional Guide

The list of natural foods suggest that we drink about a gallon of water a day to promote the mineral balance of our body. Drinking plenty of water allows the body to eliminate phlegm, mucus, toxins, and other harmful chemicals. The food guide suggests drinking natural spring water. I have no problem drinking natural spring water, it's natural because I want to lead a healthy life, and the spring water comes from the basement of the earth and expels many minerals before going back up on the surface. We all know that minerals are found in the soil of the earth in the depths of the subsoil, so I like to drink natural spring water.

Natural Spring Water

In the early morning, I drink spring water when I get up; it is the first liquid or food that enters my body every morning. Water awakens the glands and organs of the body and activates them according to their natural rhythmic cycles of earthly time. As you know, the body works according to the rhythm.

Natural Living Meals Upon Waking Up In The Morning

- Spring water

- Alkaline herbal teas

- Or a glass of plain warm water, or in the form of herbal tea

The Difference In Fruits And Vegetables

For breakfast, I take natural organic alkaline fruits from Dr. Sebi's nutritional guide. I learned by reading Dr. Africa's book "Holistic African Health" about the circadian rhythm of the body, which implies that it works in line with the rhythm of the body. What this means is that there is a specific moment in the body which every cell and every organ performs a different task. For example, there is a time for eating, a time for digestion, a time for cleansing, and a time for assimilation.

The difference between fruits and vegetables is that fruits help to rinse and cleanse the body while vegetables help build and regenerate cells and body tissues. Both fruits and vegetables play a role in the cleansing and regeneration of cells, but a balanced diet will allow one or the other to flourish by performing one of the tasks in a predominantly extremely satisfactory manner. Therefore, the fruits help to rinse and cleanse the waste from the body. Vegetables help balance minerals, melanin, carbon, and chlorophyll.

When To Eat Fresh Fruits

From 3 am till noon, the body eliminates and discharges waste products in the body. This is why there is plenty of urination and mucus discharge during this time. To further help the body to get rid of these wastes with ease, liquid and easily digestible foods should be eaten during these hours. These easily digestible foods purify the body since less energy is needed to process them. This is the more reason why the alkaline foods on Dr. Sebi's list should be adopted into your diet as they play an important role in expelling all kinds of waste from the body. The molecular structure of fruits complements the body, and in turn, your health gets a strong backing.

When To Eat Vegetables

From the early hours of the day until late in the evening, the body flushes wastes and toxins. To aid this process, foods that the body can easily breakdown is on the top choice in the long list of Dr. Sebi Nutritional Guide. Fruits, water, and alkaline herbal teas should also be considered.

For lunch, fresh vegetables should be considered. This kind of diet will help to balance the body's general health. After the flushing of wastes in the body, it would be unwise to feed them back into that same body. Fresh vegetables are one sure way to provide the body with the natural nutrients it needs.

CHAPTER 2

Best Ways To Get Rid Of Phlegm After Eating And Clear Mucus From The Throat

Phlegm is nothing more than a gel-like mucus that is produced by the mucus membranes, and these liquids are also expelled from the body through the lungs, bronchioles, and diaphragm. This waste is utterly disgusting and gross. Coming in contact with phlegm makes me want to puke out my lungs. Phlegm does not have a definite outlook; sometimes, it can be as clear as water; other times, it can be yellowish, green, dark, grey, pale, or brown depending on the type of foods you consume. Some think the color of phlegm discharged from your body is an indication of how healthy you are, but there is no substantial evidence to back this up yet.

Phlegm can be likened to a chameleon that will take the color of its environment. In this case, the color of the food consumed is what is considered. Mucus and phlegm are similar to the untrained eyes, but they have their differences – one is more dangerous to human health than the other. You will soon find out how this has come to be.

What is mucus?

Mucus is basically a gel-like liquid that is secreted by the mucus membranes; the texture is thick and slippery. This liquid comprises of water and glycoproteins in abundance.

Difference Between Phlegm And Mucus

Mucus and phlegm are not identical, although most people consider them to be one. Let me explain, mucus is produced by our natural body as a defense mechanism. For example, mucus traps bacteria, so they do not enter the body. But if you eat too many unnatural foods that cause excessive mucus production by your body, it will be a problem because the cells and organs will be deprived of oxygen.

Phlegm Carries Disease

On the other hand, phlegm is very difficult to expel from the body. The presence of phlegm in the body is an indication that there is a disease lurking around somewhere in the body. When phlegm is excreted in the body, mucus accompanies it as well as bacteria.

This is the more reason why phlegm is more problematic to the body.

The Relation Between Food And Disease

Mucus disease

It is ideal to know the concept of diseases, the environments where it thrives, and the causes. With this knowledge handy, it will be difficult for us to fall sick. This is the key to staying away from diseases and illnesses that your doctor will never tell you about.

When we know these things, there won't be the need for a healer as getting sick will be a rare occurrence.

Mucus Is The Cause Of Every Disease - Dr. Sebi

Diseases is found in the body when you have ingested an uncomplimentary substance into our body. This substance will conflict with our genetic structure, and this will eventually lead to us getting sick and weak. Almost everyone usually get sick due to excess mucus in the body. The cause of most diseases is the presence of excessive mucus in the body.

When mucus accumulates excessively in the body, the mucus membrane breaks down, and cells get covered by the excess mucus. In essence, the mucus membrane is to protect the body from the invasion of aerobic bacteria.

Mucus And Phlegm Cause Disease

When our diet is made up of acidic food, the mucus membrane breaks down, and the already secreted mucus gets into the bloodstream. When this happens, the other groups of cells that belong to the organs get deprived of oxygen. If the mucus travels to your nostrils, it is referred to as sinusitis, when it flows to bronchial tube, it is called bronchitis and when it enters the lungs, it is called pneumonia. If mucus manages to get into your eyes, there will be a problem with vision.

There you have it, three different diseases caused by mucus. There are more diseases; on the long list of other diseases caused by the invasion of mucus into various organs of the body are:

- Prostatitis – when mucus gets into your prostate gland

- Endometriosis – when mucus gets into the uterus of a woman (this can lead to yeast infection and vaginal discharge).

When you have the symptoms of any of these diseases, excessive mucus production caused by an inadequate diet is the underlying cause.

Phlegm After Eating

Humans experience phlegm every other time. When you cough out phlegm after eating, it is as a result of you consuming acidic food. Now you understand that the excessive acidic food that you consume is the cause of you coughing out phlegm. One of the significant factors that contribute to the excessive production of phlegm in the body is the consumption of processed foods. The body does not recognize these foods, and it in turn results in a conflict. If after eating a particular type of food, you find yourself producing a lot of phlegm via cough, you need to stay away from such food. The production of excess phlegm due to the consumption of a particular type of food is an indication that such food is unhealthy. The secretion of excessive phlegm will deprive the body of oxygen as well as other parts of your internal organs.

Symptoms Of Constant Mucus In The Throat

Acidic foods do not compliment the biological structure of the human body. The body's reaction to this is to produce more mucus every time you eat acidic foods. Excess mucus in the longs will extend to the throat. This situation will lead you to cough out phlegm after every meal you take.

A temporary solution to this condition is to gargle saltwater, but a diet change is what is needed to stop the body from producing excess mucus. If you refuse to change your diet to one that will eliminate the excessive production of phlegm, there will be more of it to cough out every time you consume acidic food. Every organ of the body that hosts this excessive mucus will experience one disease or the other.

Natural Remedies To Clear Mucus

- Go on a 2-7 days juice fast to help your body cleanse and flush out the mucus/phlegm accompanied by a mix diet of fruit and vegetables recommended by Dr. Sebi.

- Boiled a quart of water, add half tsp. of Lobelia, and let it steep. When it is lukewarm, strain it, and drink as much as you can. Stick your finger down your throat so you can vomit to clear your stomach of phlegm and mucus.

- Take a hot bath, before this, briefly make the water cold and run it on your body. Go to bed, then have someone give you a hot fomentation to your chest and spine, and completing it with a cold on - this is to relieve congestion.

- Remember, changing your diet is the most important thing you can do to help your body from producing excess phlegm and mucus.

Natural remedies for phlegm

- Hot drinks such as teas or warm water help cough out

phlegm. Coughing is the best and only way the phlegm can come out.

- Eat a variety of fruits and vegetables and make juices with them.

Anise tea and almond milk are good. Make your own almond milk (https://www.amazon.com/dp/B07XJCTLW1).Heat a pan of water or use a humidifier to add moisture in the air.

- Drink a lot of fluid: natural spring water, homemade soups, and natural herbal alkaline teas.

- Drink about 2-3 quarts of liquid a day so the phlegm can gently be expelled.

- Cayenne and lobelia will help break up congestion when swallowed

Herbs for mucus and phlegm relief

To help your body create a balance in the production of mucus and phlegm, herbs like wild cherry bark, Echinacea, slippery elm bark, chickweed, ginkgo Biloba, burdock, and lobelia should be considered as an essential part of your diet. For more herbs that can help your situation, get my book on Dr. Sebi Approved Herbs here: (https://www.amazon.com/dp/B07TYPSRFF).

Mucusless Diet And Mucus Relief

Avoid eating the following to help your body from producing excessive phlegm and mucus:

- White-flour and white sugar are highly processed acidic foods which increase mucus and phlegm

- Phlegm after eating eggs is due to the excessive mucus it creates in the body; it is difficult for the body to breakdown a fetus, which is what eggs are.

- Phlegm after eating sugar is to the highly processed and artificial sweetener has to breakdown and protects itself.

- Do not use milk, which produces thick phlegm and hinder healing

- Phlegm after eating yogurt is due to dairy, which produces excessive thick phlegm in the body.

- Phlegm after eating bread is due to the processed, dairy, and acidic ingredients such as white flour, eggs, white sugar, or GMO grains.

- Phlegm after eating dairy is due to the thick phlegm and excess mucus dairy products produce in the body.

- Stop smoking and get tobacco out of your home

Phlegm and mucus are not to be toyed with, as leaving them unattended can lead to diseases like pneumonia, lung congestion, acute bronchitis, chronic bronchitis, and bronchiectasis. This highlighted guide should be followed keenly in order to get rid of excess mucus and phlegm in the body as the production of these two in excess ultimately lead to diseases. Get a copy of Dr. Sebi's nutritional guide to clean and flush phlegm as well as mucus out of your body here (https://www.amazon.com/dp/B07RXLZ8VN).

CHAPTER 3

Benefits of fasting as recommended by Dr. Sebi

Some set of individuals wait until they get sick before they embark on a fasting journey while others fast before they get sick as a preventive measure to never getting sick — people who fast have now been grouped into two.

Preventive fast is a prudent step to boosting the body's immune system to combat every disease infection. This is also effective against lesser-known diseases, which may cause a lot of pain. Fasting after getting sick is to eliminate undesirable health conditions after a disease must have taken over in the body.

Following the example that has been put in place by Mother Nature, a once in a year spring cleansing comes to mind, and this is similar to preventive fast detoxification. Flushing, detoxing and cleansing the body of its impurities that have manifested and those that are yet to manifest.

No doubt, fasting is nature's best healing mechanism as it allows every organ of the body to activate its natural healing abilities. When the body is not at ease, it has a tendency to lose its appetite. This is an indication that fasting is nature's best principle of self-healing.

Fasting benefits the body in the sense that accumulated wastes, toxins, and impurities are effectively removed. In most cases, these impurities attract diseases to them, and fasting is the best preventive measure for these diseases. When suffering from any of these illnesses, fasting is the best way to tackle them.

Fasting will improve your general health due to the following reasons;

- The respiratory organs, throat, chest, bronchial asthma, pneumonia all benefit from fasting. The health benefits of fasting are astronomical. Not only is it a useful spiritual tool in much sacred religious texts, fasting is universal, meaning it does not change. It is one of the 7 laws to good health.

- When you go to China, India, or Africa, fasting endures. It's everlasting because it hasn't changed since fasting is among air, water, sunlight, and countless other mineral dust which were here since day one.

- Menopausal symptoms, chronic inflammation of the womb, benign tumors of female sex organs, fallopian tube and ovary, and menstrual flow regularity can all be eliminated by fasting.

- Fasting eliminates diseases of the digestive organs, bowels, and catarrh of the stomach, liver and gall bladder infections, and constipation.

- Fasting will eradicate skin diseases such as eczema, nettle rash, sensitive skin, acne, and boils.

- Diseases of the heart, blood vessels circulation, coronary thrombosis, low or high blood pressure, and bloodstream congestion and lymphatic system are eased as a result of fasting.

- Fast for hot flushes, plethora, beginning cases of

arteriosclerosis, after-effects of phlebitis or thrombosis, and aging.

- Kidney and bladder diseases, like nephritis, vesical, pyelitis, and renal calculus, are eliminated by fasting.

Fasting can help fix metabolism of chronic underweight and obesity, rheumatism in the muscles and joints, diabetes before it gets too advanced, and sciatica. Fast for blood changes due to nicotine, alcohol, arsenic, mercury, sleeping pills, and prescription drugs during the new effects or not yet advance in stages. The preventive fast can help with diseases due to blood changes that can cause chronic inflammation or tonsils suppuration in the middle ear.

Fasting is helpful for nervous complaints like exhaustion, migraine, recurring headache, neuralgia, insomnia, depression, and neuritis.

According to Dr. Afrika, " There is a time to take, a time to give and a time to receive." Hippocrates, in his words, admonished everyone to practice abstinence for thy health, thy well-being, and thy days be numbered. Every human is a healer and that healing ability is activated through fasting.

CHAPTER 4

Foods During Fasting

Dr. Sebi has recommended foods that are easy to digest and ones that will push the body's performance to its peak.

Basically, fasting is abstinence from food, and this act greatly improves the elimination of waste materials from the body. Pollution, environmental toxins, synthetic medication, electrical radiation are all forms of things we take that can diminish our overall health. Fasting is a mechanism that speedily removes toxins like mucus, fecal waste, parasites, and phlegm from the body.

What Type Of Fasting Foods To Eat

The world-renowned doctor, Dr. Sebi, recommends that if you have to eat during a fast for medical reasons, you must know the right combinations of food to eat that will further aid the elimination of wastes and toxins. It is more advantageous to eat natural alkaline fruits, vegetables, and freshly made juices from these fruits.

#1 To provide the elements that your body needs during a fast, there is a need to eat foods that are rich in minerals and can be easily broken down and digested by the body. This diet will ensure that your body has excess energy to expel waste materials before beginning its healing process.

Dr. Sebi Fasting Foods Checklist

Here are the benefits of Dr. Sebi's fasting food; these are the benefits to your body when you eat the recommended fasting foods. Natural foods all contain 92 minerals found in the soil of the earth, 27 of which are found and play an important role in the human body to restore good health and bring our body back to its original state of health. These foods contain the following benefits that are essential for the optimal and proper functioning of the body.

The fasting foods provide:

- Alkalinity

- Iron, calcium, magnesium, copper, zinc, and many other minerals

- Expel mucus

- Easy to digest, assimilate, and used by the body

- They flush out the body and detox harmful wastes

- Neutralize the body's PH balance

- Restore the body overall good health

- Get rid of toxins

The Fasting Foods To Eat

Fruits:

- Seeded melons

- Mangoes

- All types of berries

- Papaya and many more, there is a complete list of these fruits in my other book

(book link already provided in chapter two above)

Vegetables to eat during fasting?

If you have to eat during your fast for medical reasons or any other situation you are in.

These vegetables are ideal for consumption because of their ability to help the body expel mucus or toxins due to their high mineral content:

- Dandelion leaves

- Green leafy vegetables

- Kale

- Broth of burdock leaf, or root vegetable juices.

For more information on alkaline vegetables, see the natural foods guide in the previous chapters. Dr. Sebi used these foods to remove mucus and other body wastes from his body system.

CHAPTER 5

How To Fast Safely To Remove Mucus, Toxins, And Lose Weight

What Is Fasting?

The best way to safely fast is the question on the lips of many. Before we delve into that, there is a need to paint a clearer picture of what fasting is. Abstinence from food totally or partially for some reason is what is regarded as fasting. According to Dr. Alvenia Fulton, "The best juices are fresh juices made from your blender out of fresh fruits and vegetables, not from canned or frozen foods."

Before you fast

#1. Fasting comes in two phases in order to cleanse your body effectively. Firstly, you have to cleanse your body with natural herbs for at least five days before embarking on the actual fasting.

#2. To know when you are ready for the fast, your body will give an indication of that, and the indication you are going to get is during the cleansing with herbs phase. When you start feeling hungry while cleansing is when you are truly ready to begin your fast. You should never fast when your body is not ready, if you feel hungry during a fast, you should eat.

Why should you fast

If you want to know how to correct your body's discomforts, fasting will fix your body and keep you younger. The best method of fasting is to clean the body until there is no more hunger. When there is no hunger, you can fast as long as you like. Fast until your appetite returns because it will disappear. The tongue will become white and soft; fast until the tongue turns red again, and fast until your breath and your body become sweet. The body will produce its own smell due to the removal of all the toxic waste in the body.

What fasting will do

You will look younger, feel younger, skin rejuvenated, and your hair and nails will be revitalized. Fasting will do all these things in your body. If you fast, your body will remain flexible, full of energy, and shine with vitality. This is what we all want, and nothing will do that better than cleansing and fasting. Nothing will do a better job at healing, developing, and relieving our body of waste and toxins if not for fasting (juice, vegetable, or water fasting).

What about Water fasting

Fasting with water is better because it will clean the body of toxic waste, heal the body of old dead cells that have been there for a long time. The best way to do this is to cleanse the body and then start the water fast. When you fast, you will find that your skin becomes resonant, young, and beautiful. Your hair, your eyes, and every gland in your body will respond to fasting. This is what they all need, the intense cleansing that occurs from fasting. If you fast, your friends or people you know can say that you are killing yourself. But I did not listen to them; even during biblical days, people fasted for 21, 30, or 40 days, and no one died of fasting. The prophets, Jesus and the women of the Bible, fasted, and no one died for it. Queen Esther fasted and saved the children of Israel from extinction. Fasting is a way of life.

How to prepare for fasting

Your fasting should start with cleansing. Use different natural herbs for 3 to 5 days before starting your fast, be it a juice, a vegetable, or water fast. Take herbs first to remove some of the toxin and body waste. Most people have toxins that have been in their bodies since they were babies, so herbs are very important before any type of fasting. For example, the first time I tried fasting, on the 21st day, I could not get up quickly enough to go to the bathroom because I had a lot of toxins coming out of me. I am glad because what keeps us alive is cleansing and eliminating waste and toxins from the body.

How long should you fast?

After cleaning the body with herbs, fast for 21 or 30 days until you no longer have a "coated" tongue, you no longer feel tired, weak, or nervous and you feel young again. The people around you are going to ask you what you are doing; you will look more youthful. Then, break the fast and begin again; if you cleanse the body quickly and adequately, you do not need to take drug to do what you want. Male or female, your sex drive will continue to work well, and your hormones will work if they are cleansed and quickly.

Fast to cleanse toxins

You will come to the realization that what keeps us alive as humans are not food. What keeps us alive is getting rid of toxins and waste in our body. When we consume what nature has provided us with, and we fast to cleanse our body on top of that, our body and mind will change.

Our ancestors do not have prostate glands problems like the young men of nowadays. Our grandmothers as well did not lose their youthful factor as it is in today's world. As a matter of fact, my great grandmother had twin babies at the age of 49, but this is unheard of in the 21st century despite all the medical discoveries. When we eat according to what nature has in store for us, we will stay healthy, live longer, and every pain in the body will vanish. Good health will ultimately triumph when we cleanse our body and stick to the right diet.

How do you break a fast

You are to break a fast exactly the way you started. By this, I mean, get a juice, warm it up and take that for 5 consecutive days. You will have more energy than you need. You won't feel hungry. If you jump right into taking steaks after an extensive fasting period, you will get sick.

That food will make you fall ill. You have to totally stop all those kinds of food as they cause body pains and ache. You did not come to this world to live a short life. There are so many ways to fast. The aim of this guide and information therein is to know the correct way for you to fast. In the end, this is all about choosing a fasting method that works well for you.

Conclusion

Lastly, as one of my most favorable readers, your feedback is of the utmost importance to me, this book and other readers. I am always resolute to offer the best experience for my readers, and your input helps me to define that experience. That being said, if you could take a minute to post a REVIEW on this book here on this platform, I would so much appreciate it.

Hope to see you again soon!

Carin

Other Books By Carin C. Hendry

DR. SEBI CURE FOR HERPES: *A Simple Guide On How To Cure Herpes Simplex Virus Using Dr. Sebi Alkaline Diet Eating Method*

https://www.amazon.com/dp/B07WVR8H6W

DR. SEBI DETOX CLEANSE: *Revitalize Yourself With Dr. Sebi Mucus Cleansing Alkaline Diet By Adopting An Alkaline Diet Through Dr. Sebi*

https://www.amazon.com/dp/B07XJCTLW1

DR. SEBI INSPIRED DETOX

NUTRITIONAL GUIDE:
Adopting An Alkaline Diet Through Dr. Sebi Approved Food List And Herbs

https://www.amazon.com/dp/B07RXLZ8VN

DR. SEBI APPROVED HERBS: *Cleanse, Heal and Revitalize Your Body With Dr. Sebi Herbs by Adopting an Alkaline Diet through Dr. Sebi*
https://www.amazon.com/dp/B07TYPSRFF

DR. SEBI APPROVED 12 DAY SMOOTHIE DETOX GUIDE: *12 Delicious Dr. Sebi Smoothie Recipes to Cleanse and Revitalize Your Body by Following an Alkaline Diet Through Dr. Sebi Nutritional Guide*
https://www.amazon.com/dp/B07SQR1KK7

DR. SEBI: *How to Naturally Detox the Liver, Reverse Diabetes and High Blood Pressure Through Dr. Sebi Alkaline Diet*
https://www.amazon.com/dp/B07TW3MT5W

DIRTY LAZY KETO: *The Complete Beginner Guide On Ketogenic Diet For Weight Loss Using Keto Diet Recipes*
https://www.amazon.com/dp/B07SRKBLBM

KETOSIS STRIPS: *The Complete User Guide To Using Keto Test Strips To Measure Ketone Levels In Urine And Blood And Getting Into Ketosis Faster*

https://www.amazon.com/dp/B07S6GQFTL

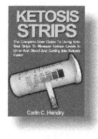

CELERY JUICE: *A simplified guide to the benefits, weight loss practice and healing powers of celery juice smoothies*
https://www.amazon.com/dp/B07T2RTS13

WEIGHT LOSS JOURNEY: *A Step By Step Guide To Lose Belly Fat And Body Weight FAST!*
https://www.amazon.com/dp/B07N7SX4N3

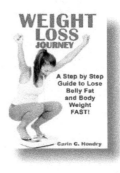

Thanks For Reading

CPSIA information can be obtained
at www.ICGtesting.com
Printed in the USA
BVHW061108220820
587017BV00004B/5